*Jane Austen Dictionary*

# *Jane Austen Dictionary*

A Guide to the Language
in Jane Austen's Novels

Pauline E. Kelly

*InkWell Publishing*
*Arlington, MA*

© 2009 by Pauline E. Kelly

All rights reserved. This book or parts thereof, may not be reproduced or transmitted in any form or by any means electronic or mechanical including recording, photocopying or any information storage and retrieval system without the written permission of the author.

Published by

InkWell Publishing
Arlington, MA

ISBN 978-0-9768812-3-0

Printed in the United States of America

*for Cathy*

*I have lost such a sister,
such a friend, as can never
have been surpassed...*
   *Cassandra Austen*

*Northanger Abbey*

*Sense and Sensibility*

*Pride and Prejudice*

*Emma*

*Mansfield Park*

*Persuasion*

# Acknowledgements

The idea for this book took shape at the first meeting of my Jane Austen's Book and Film Club. I arrived with a list of unusual and puzzling words, together with their meanings, to share with the group. My niece, Heather Mariacher, was the first to suggest this list could be useful to many people, and should be made into a book. Another member of the group, Lori Lee Souder, who is an expert in vintage clothing, was able to add interesting and esoteric information about the clothing and fabrics on the list. And so to these book club members and friends I am most grateful.

Thank you to my wonderful editor and special friend, Scott Heidemann, not only for his eagle eye, but also for his thoughtful criticism, helpful suggestions, and enthusiastic support.

Thank you to Jack Boyce for his beautiful cover design, which greatly adds to the overall appeal of the book.

I am very grateful to Pia Frauss for permission to use her beautiful Jane Austen font, which provides enhanced enjoyment when reading the quotes.

# Introduction

Reading a Jane Austen novel is always a great pleasure, but many of the words that were popular in Regency England have become obscure in this century, often describing items or practices that no longer exist. In addition, the way in which words were used 200 years ago has changed, giving the modern day reader pause.

We may wonder exactly what a person was wearing when they donned a pelisse or a great coat, and how a barouche differed from a gig as a mode of transportation. Or we may think it strange that people went about "quizzing" people at social gatherings, without realizing that quizzing meant teasing in Jane Austen's time.

This book is designed to answer some of these questions, while providing an enjoyable look into the times in which Jane Austen wrote. It is not meant as a scholarly work, but rather as an informative and entertaining reference.

**abroad** Out of one's house; out in the open air.

*The storm too abroad so dreadful!*
— Northanger Abbey

**acrostic** A poem or other writing in which the first letter, syllable, or word of the line spells out a name or other message.

> Names were popular acrostics, and would-be poets would attempt to gain favor with ladies by writing a poem using the letters in the woman's name as the acrostic, such as Mrs. Elton received in *Emma*. The poem on the following page, written by Lewis Carroll, spells out the name of Alice Pleasance Liddell, the

inspiration for the character of Alice in his books, *Alice in Wonderland* and *Through the Looking Glass*.

A boat beneath a sunny sky,
Lingering onward dreamily
In an evening of July –
Children three that nestle near,
Eager eye and willing ear,
Pleased a simple tale to hear –
Long had paled that sunny sky:
Echoes fade and memories die.
Autumn frosts have slain July.
Still she haunts me, phantomwise,
Alice moving under skies
Never seen by waking eyes.
Children yet, the tale to hear,
Eager eye and willing ear,
Lovingly shall nestle near.
In a Wonderland they lie,
Dreaming as the days go by,
Dreaming as the summers die:
Ever drifting down the stream –
Lingering in the golden gleam –
Life, what is it but a dream?

Another example of an acrostic is the following children's poem where the three initial letters of each line spell out abbreviations for the months of the year:

Janet was quite ill one day.

Febrile trouble came her way.

Martyr-like, she lay in bed;

Aproned nurses softly sped.

Maybe, said the leech judicial

Junket would be beneficial.

Juleps, too, though freely tried,

August ill, for Janet died.

Sepulcher was sadly made.

Octaves pealed and prayers
  were said.

Novices with ma'y a tear

Decorated Janet's bier.

— Anonymous

# A

**address** The manner of presenting yourself; to raise oneself; to stand erect.

> *His address was good, and Catherine felt herself in high luck.*
>
> —Northanger Abbey

**amor patriae** Love of one's country. Latin.

**apothecary** A general medical practitioner whose training was through apprenticeship. He sold drugs and occasionally made house calls and dispensed advise, although he was only permitted to charge for the drugs and not the advice. Since he sold drugs, he was a considered a tradesman, and therefore had no social standing.

**apprehension** Understanding.

> *The Kellynch property was good, but not equal to Sir Walter's apprehension of the state required in its possessor.*
>
> —Persuasion

**arch** Mischievous, roguish; clever or slyly alert, an arch glance.

> —Oh! That arch eye of yours!—It sees through everything.
> —Northanger Abbey

**archness** Cleverness, good-natured slyness, mischievous irony.

> He talked with fluency and spirit—and there was an archness and pleasantry in his manner which interested, though it was hardly understood by her.
> —Northanger Abbey

**arrangé** Artificial.

> I used to think she had some taste in dress, but I was ashamed of her at the concert. Something so formal and arrangé in her air!
> —Persuasion

**assizes** Country court sessions.

Most county cases were handled by the local constable or justice of the peace, however, those that were too difficult or too serious were presided over by circuit-riding judges. These sessions were scheduled to occur twice a year, and were important occasions for the people in the county. When the circuit judge arrived, a banquet would be held for the notables. Judging took place the following day.

**au fait** In the know.

> One likes to hear what is going on, to be au fait as to the newest modes of being trifling and silly.
>
> —Persuasion

**awful** Awe-inspiring.

> Its long, damp passages, its narrow cells and ruined chapel, were to be within her daily reach, and she could not entirely subdue the hope of some traditional legends, some awful memorials of an injured and ill-fated nun.
>
> —Northanger Abbey

**backed** (referring to a horse)  Ridden or broken to the saddle.

> *I would give any money for a real good hunter. I have three now, the best that ever were back'd.*
>
> — Northanger Abbey

**baited**  A feed for horses; fed.

> *...when the horses were baited, he was off.*
>
> — Persuasion

**banns** The public notice given in a church of a couple's intention to marry, in order that those who know of any impediment or objection may have the opportunity of voicing their objections.

Before a marriage could take place, the local clergyman would announce from the pulpit their intended plans for three consecutive Sundays during the service, thereby "publishing the banns." If no one objected, the couple could be married within 90 days of the final announcement. A marriage license was not

required, however, people with financial means usually did purchase a license from a clergyman, which allowed them to marry in the parish where either the bride or groom had resided for at least 15 days.

A special license could be obtained for special circumstances, such as wanting to marry in a parish where neither the bride nor groom resided, marrying without publishing the banns, or marrying during holy seasons when the church prohibited marriages. The special license was issued by the Archbishop of Canterbury, and cost between four and five pounds, thus making it prohibitive, except for the very wealthy (or the very desperate).

**barouche** (pronounced "ba-roosh") A four-wheeled, horse-drawn carriage with a collapsible top that folded back, two double seats inside facing each other, and a box seat outside in front for the driver. It was usually pulled by four horses in pairs, and was generally owned by those in the higher social circles, as caring for four horses was expensive. From the Latin *birotus*: bi, two; *rota*, wheel; Italian *biroccio*; German *Barutsche*.

barouche

**barouche-landau** While the ordinary barouche had a collapsible cover in the back and covered the passengers seated in the rear when opened, the barouche-laudau had a collapsible cover in the front and the back, covering all passengers when raised.

The landau carriage takes its name from Landau, Bavaria (in what is now West Germany), where it was first made, probably as early as the seventeenth century. The landau was a full-size carriage accommodating four or six passengers on two full-width seats, the rear one facing forward and the front one facing aft. All early carriages were essentially open models that gradually developed into enclosed models to protect the riders from rain and cold. The landau was distinctive in being an enclosed carriage with a top that could be folded down (in essence, the first "convertible"). The top was made in two sections so that one part folded forward and the other folded back.

barouche landau

**bass** In musical notation, a shorthand method of indicating harmony; also, the study of harmony.

*They found Mary, as usual, deep in the study of thorough bass and human nature; and had some new extracts to admire, and some new observations of thread-bare morality to listen to.*

—Pride and Prejudice

**Bath**  A city in southwest England, famous for its hot springs.

>The city of Bath first drew attention from the hot springs that have been bubbling up from the ground for at least 100,000 years. The springs arise from water which percolates down through limestone aquifers to a depth of 14,000 feet where it is heated. Under pressure, the heated water rises to the surface along fissures and faults at a temperature of 120 degrees Fahrenheit at the rate of about 500,000 gallons every day.
>
>The Celts were the first to worship at the main spring, building a shrine dedicated to the goddess Sulis (the Roman equivalent of Minerva, also known as Athena). Around 60-70 AD, the Romans built a temple, and named the city Aquae Sulis (the waters of Sulis). They created the baths by

fortifying the perimeter of the main spring with oak piles, then surrounding it with stone chambers lined with lead. In the 2nd century, the spring was enclosed within a wooden barrel-vaulted building which housed a hot, warm, and cold bath. But after the withdrawal of the Romans at the beginning of the 5th century, the baths fell into disrepair, and were eventually lost as silt caved in to the structures.

It only became utilized again as a spa in 1702 when Queen Anne visited it, bringing the English nobility with her. Then, beginning in 1738, Bath itself was virtually rebuilt by the renown architect, John Wood, who created a new Georgian city by designing elegant buildings in the Palladian style. Much of the stone that was used for construction came from limestone from the mines of Combe Down and Bathampton Down. The golden, honey color of the stone gives the city a warm, mellow, and indefinable quality.

Jane Austen lived in Bath with her parents and sister from 1801 to 1806 in four different residences. Her novels, *Northanger Abbey* and *Persuasion* are largely set in the city, with many descriptions of the activities and social events revolving around the baths.

**Bath stove**  Cast-iron stove used to heat rooms.

*B*

**bathing machine** Small huts for changing into bathing attire that were wheeled to the shore, or driven a few feet into the water led by a horse. They had a rope attached to them for holding onto while the waves washed over the bather.

**benefices** A tenured, ecclesiastical appointment as rector or vicar, providing a livelihood from tithes. In most country churches, the principal landowner had the right to offer or sell these livings. From the Latin *beneficium*, benefit.

**bespeak** (or bespoke) Requested or ordered. Also, to ask a favor, such as "bespeak a dance."

*... (they) bespoke an early dinner.*
—Northanger Abbey

**bilious fever** Fever believed to be caused by a liver disorder.

## B

**black gentleman** The Devil.

> ...for she is as impatient as the black gentleman when any thing is to be done.
>
> —Emma

**blains** Blisters or sores; a skin swelling; a blotch. (Also see chilblains.)

**Bond street** A fashionable shopping street in the west end of London.

**Bonomi, Joseph** (1739-1808) An Italian architect who moved to London in 1767, and became famous for his work in England, including Southampton, where Jane Austen lived for a time.

**bottoms** Low lands or valleys.

> "It is a beautiful country," he replied; "but these bottoms must be dirty in winter."
>
> —Sense and Sensibility

**Boulanger** A brisk French country dance in which couples face each other in a line.

**bow** Curved window.

**brawn** A jellied loaf or sausage made from the fleshy part or muscle of a hog or boar. The meat was boiled, pickled and potted.

**breeches-ball** A ball of white soap rubbed over stains or marks on servants' breeches to restore whiteness.

**brickbat** Any hard object such as a brick used as a missile.

**Brighton** A seaside town approximately forty-five miles south of London.

Brighton became fashionable as a seaside resort during the mid-18th century. The medicinal use of bathing or emersion in seawater began to gain popularity during this time, drawing tourists and those seeking health benefits to the small fishing village. By 1780, Georgian terraces began to flourish, and the city took on a more cosmopolitan atmosphere.

Because of its coastal location, Brighton was vulnerable to French invasion, and sailors and militia were frequently stationed there. In Jane Austen's time, Brighton gained a reputation as being somewhat risqué because of the number of off-duty sailors who were keen to enjoy themselves with liquor and ladies. In addition, George III's son, the Prince Regent, who was known for his sexual escapades, made Brighton his seaside home, building The Prince's Royal Pavilion, furthering Brighton's reputation as a place for romantic trysts.

**bustle** An uproar. To move or cause to move energetically and busily. An excited and often noisy activity; a stir.

> *Well, remember that it is not my fault, if we set all the old ladies in Bath in a bustle.*
>
> — Northanger Abbey

**cant** Hypocritically pious language. Monotonous talk filled with insincere platitudes.

> "I am no novel reader — I seldom look into novels — Do not imagine that I often read novels — It is really very well for a novel." Such is the common cant.
>
> —Northanger Abbey

***cara sposo*** Dear husband. Italian.

# C

**cassino (or casino)** Popular card game for two to four people in which players seek to score eleven by combining cards in the hand with those revealed on the table.

**caviler** One who raises petty or frivolous objections, finds fault unfairly or without good reason, or raises trivial objections. To quibble. From the Latin *cavillari*, to hear.

**chair** An enclosed sedan or light one-horse vehicle. It can also refer to an enclosed "chair" (or sedan chair) carried on two poles by servants. It was a popular way for ladies to be transported to a ball.

> ...she cheerfully submitted to the wish of Mr. Allen, which took them rather early away, and her spirits danced within her, as she danced in her chair all the way home.
>
> — Northanger Abbey

*C*

**chaise** A two-wheeled enclosed carriage drawn by one horse, often with a collapsible hood, and seating three. Variant of Old French, *chaiere*, chair.

> *We three shall be able to go very well in my chaise; and when we are in town, if you do not like to go wherever I do, well and good, you may always go with one of my daughters.*
> —Sense and Sensibility

chaise

# C

**chaise and four** Four-wheeled pleasure carriage seating up to three people, and pulled by four horses.

chaise and four

**chandler** One who makes or sells candles. Chandler shops often sold soap as well. From the Latin, *candela*, candle.

*Catherine was ashamed to say how pretty she thought it, as the General seemed to think an apology necessary for the flatness of the country, and the size of the*

> village; but in her heart she preferred it to any place she had ever been at, and looked with great admiration at every neat house above the rank of a cottage, and all the little chandler's shops which they passed.
>
> — Northanger Abbey

**character** Reputation.

**chariot** A fancy, four-horse vehicle for four people who faced front rather than facing each other, and fitted with a coach box.

> ...on hearing a carriage drive up to the door, she went to the window to see who could be coming so unreasonably early, she was all astonishment to perceive Mrs. Jennings's chariot, which she knew had not been ordered till one.
>
> — Sense and Sensibility

# C

**checked** (in reference to a horse) Reined-in.

> ...the horse was immediately checked with a violence which almost threw him on his haunches, and the servant having now scampered up, the gentleman jumped out, and the equipage was delivered to his care.
> — Northanger Abbey

**chilblains** Mild form of frostbite from over-exposure to cold, in which the hands, feet, or ears swell, followed by an itchy irritation.

**chimney-board** A board or screen placed in front of the fireplace during the summer months.

> And I am sure Lucy would have done just the same by me; for a year or two back, when Martha Sharpe and I had so many secrets together, she never made any bones of hiding in a closet, or behind a chimney-board, on purpose to hear what we said.
> — Sense and Sensibility

**circulating library** A type of lending-library at a time when public libraries did not exist.

In Jane Austen's time, books were often very expensive, and free lending libraries for the public had not yet come into existence. Families seeking reading materials would subscribe to a circulating library through an annual fee. One of the most popular of these libraries was that of Charles Edward Mundine, which was in existence from 1842-1894, and which exerted enormous influence over the kinds of books that were published.

*By degrees the girls came to spend the chief of the morning upstairs, at first only in working and talking; but after a few days, the remembrance of the said books grew so potent and stimulative, that Fanny found it impossible not to try for books again. There were none in her father's house; but wealth is luxurious and daring; and*

# C

*some of hers found its way to a circulating library. She became a subscriber; amazed at being anything in propia persona, amazed at her own doings in every way; to be a renter, a chooser of books! And to be having any one's improvement in view in her choice! But so it was. Susan had read nothing, and Fanny longed to give her a share in her own first pleasures, and inspire a taste for the biography and poetry which she delighted in herself.*

—Mansfield Park

**(the) Cobb** Stone breakwater that bordered the harbor in Lyme and provided a place to walk along the sea.

**cockade** An ornament, such as a knot of ribbons or rosette worn on a hat or shoe. It was often a badge or part of livery dress.

**combe** (pronouned "coom") A short valley or hollow on a hill or coastline. Combes are generally dry valleys in a limestone or chalk escarpment.

**coming out** Public recognition that a young girl was ready to assume the demeanor and responsibilities of adulthood, and available for marriage. It was often marked by a formal social event given in her honor.

The official coming out ceremony for young women of society took place at approximately 16 years of age when they were presented to the sovereign at court, making them officially a member of society, and thus officially available for marriage. It was a major right of passage for a young girl, as she moved from being essentially invisible socially, to being in the center of a whirlwind of balls, dances, and festive social occasions. The goal of all this social activity was to be noticed and ultimately married within a season or two.

The ceremony took place at the Court of St. James in a formal drawing room. The debutant was required to wear a train exactly three feet long, and feathers were placed at the back of her head, high enough to be visible to Her Majesty when the lady entered the room. Her neck and shoulders must be bare. At the appointed time, she approached the throne, her train having been spread out by an attendant, and a card bearing her name was handed to a lord-in-waiting, who announced

her to Her Majesty. The lady then curtsied, kissed the hand of the Queen, arose, curtseyed once more, and backed out of the room, not turning her face away from the Queen.

**commerce** (card game)  A popular card game, similar to poker, in which players barter cards with one another in an attempt to get three of a kind, a straight, flush, etc.

**complaisance**  Affability, desire to please. The inclination to comply willingly with the wishes of others; amiability.

**concert bill**  A program at a concert.

**confined**  About to give birth.

**conjurer**  A clever person.

*...poor Nancy, who, you know, is a well-meaning creature, but no conjurer.*

— Sense and Sensibility

**connexions**  Relations, or extended kin.

**consequences** (parlor game)  A round game involving drawing conclusions from a name or a fact, without knowing the entire conversation.

*They met for the sake of eating, drinking, and laughing together, playing at cards, or consequences, or any other game that was sufficiently noisy.*
— Sense and Sensibility

**conservatory** A room in a country house, usually facing east, with floor to ceiling windows that capitalized on the sun in a time when central heating did not exist. It was used to grow indoor plants.

**Constantia wine** A sweet wine made at Constantia Farm near Cape Town, South Africa.

**coppice or copse** A thicket or grove of small trees or shrubs, maintained by periodic cutting or pruning.

*They determined on walking round Beechan Cliff, that noble hill, whose beautiful verdure and hanging coppice render it so striking an object from almost every opening in Bath.*
— Northanger Abbey

**coquelicot** (pronounced "co-key-li-cot") The color of the common red poppy, a brilliant red with a tint of orange. Coquelicot means poppy in French.

> Do you know, I saw the prettiest hat you can imagine, in a shop window in Milsom-street just now — very like yours, only with coquelicot ribbons instead of green; I quite longed for it.
> — Northanger Abbey

**coquette** Flirt. A woman who makes teasing sexual or romantic overtures.

> Coquette means "little cock." The domestic cock is noted for his arrogant (or cocky) strut, and for his promiscuity. A Frenchman who displayed similar amorousness and swagger earned the nickname of coquet, a diminutive of coq, "rooster." Coquette is the feminine form of coquet.

> *I see what she has been about. She is a vain coquette, and her tricks have not answered.*
>
> —Northanger Abbey

**cordial** A cheerful remark; warm and sincere, friendly. From the Latin *cor*, cord-, heart.

> *With this parting cordial she curtseys off — you listen to the sound of her receding footsteps as long as the last echo can reach you — and when, with fainting spirits, you attempt to fasten your door, you discover, with increased alarm, that it has no lock.*
>
> —Northanger Abbey

**countenance** To give sanction or support to; tolerate or approve; give moral support.

**counterpane** A bedspread; a cover for a bed with a raised design; a stitched quilt. From the Latin *culcita* (quilt) and *puncta* (to sew).

# C

**court-plaister** Silk-based skin covering applied to minor cuts or bruises; an early form of an adhesive bandage.

**cousin** A relative or kinsman.

**covert** Thicket or hiding place for game.

**Cowper, William** (1731-1800) Popular English nature poet who wrote about everyday life and scenes of the English countryside. He is considered the precursor of Romanticism, and was one of Jane Austen's favorite writers.

**coxcomb** A conceited fool; a fob.

Jesters' caps were called coxcombs because the points resembled the comb or crest of a cock. The word later came to mean a foolish person.

*He is the greatest coxcomb I ever saw, and amazingly disagreeable.*
— Northanger Abbey

**crape**  An alternate spelling of crepe; a soft, thin, light fabric with a finely crinkled surface. A piece of black crepe was worn as a token of mourning.

**cravats**  A scarf or fine cloth worn by men around the neck in a bow; the forerunner of the modern, tailored necktie.

> *I always buy my own cravats, and am allowed to be an excellent judge; and my sister has often trusted me in the choice of a gown.*
> —Northanger Abbey

**crescent of the day**  Early afternoon.

> *The Clifton scheme had been deferred, not relinquished, and on the afternoon's crescent of this day, it was brought forward again.*
> —Northanger Abbey

**Cromer**  Spa and vacation resort on the coast of England's North Sea.

**crown lands**  Land owned by the monarch.

**curacy** The position occupied by a curate, who assisted the vicar of the parish.

**curricle** A light, open, two-wheeled carriage, drawn by two horses abreast. Two horses made it faster than the gig, and it was therefore considered more sporty. From the Latin *curriculum*, course, and *currere*, to run.

curricle

**curricle-hung** Suspended by a pole, rather than a shaft, like the open two-wheeled horse-drawn carriage known as a curricle.

**cutting** A type of behavior done to slight or ignore someone. It was a hurtful gesture for the recipient, and could be done by merely slightly acknowledging the presence of someone who is familiar.

**cypher** (also cipher) Interwoven initials; a design combining or interweaving letters or initials; a type of monogram. Conversely, decipher means to unscramble or decode.

**dab chick** A small swimming and diving waterfowl.

*If one happens only to shut the door a little hard, she starts and wriggles like a young dab chick in the water.*

—Persuasion

## D

**debts of honour** Personal debts owed to peers. They were often acquired by gambling, and were considered more serious for gentlemen than debts owed to merchants. Repayment was not enforceable by law, and the lender would therefore have to rely on the honor of the borrower to repay them.

> Colonel Forster believed that more than a thousand pounds would be necessary to clear his expenses at Brighton. He owed a good deal in the town, but his debts of honour were still more formidable.
>
> —Pride and Prejudice

**deedily** Busily; done with great attention.

**demesne** (pronounced "di-main") The grounds belonging to a country house.

> It was a pleasant fertile spot, well wooded, and rich in pasture. After winding along it for more than a mile, they reached their own house. A small green court was

*the whole of its demesne in front; and a neat wicket gate admitted them into it.*

— Sense and Sensibility

**deputation** Privilege of shooting game on an estate.

The only people allowed to hunt game were the aristocracy and the gentry, a law established in 1671 and that existed until 1831. However, you could "deputize" a friend or neighbor to hunt game on your property.

**devoir** An act or expression of respect or courtesy; civility. Often used in the plural: pay one's devoirs. From the Latin *debere*, to owe.

*...and to her his devoirs were speedily paid, with a mixture of joy and embarrassment which might have informed Catherine,*

## D

*had she been more expert in the development of other people's feelings, and less simply engrossed by her own, that her brother thought her friend quite as pretty as she could do herself.*

— Northanger Abbey

**dimity** A sheer, crisp cotton fabric with raised woven stripes or checks, used chiefly for curtains and dresses.

*She saw a large, well-proportioned apartment, an handsome dimity bed, arranged as unoccupied with an housemaid's care, a bright Bath stove, mahogany wardrobes and neatly-painted chairs, on which the warm beams of a western sun gaily poured through two sash windows!*

— Northanger Abbey

**direction**  A street address.

> *I would write to him myself, but I have mislaid his direction.*
> —Northanger Abbey

**dishabille**  Not wearing full uniform; the state of being partially or very casually dressed; lounging attired; an intentionally careless manner. From the French, *deshabiller*, to undress.

**douceur** (pronounced "dow-sur")  A pleasant or conciliatory speech or gesture; sweetness of manner; agreeable.

> *The impertinence of these kind of scrutinizes, moreover, was generally concluded with a compliment, which, though meant as its douceur, was considered by Marianne as the greatest impertinence of all; for after undergoing an examination into the value and make of her gown, the colour of*

# D

*her shoes, and the arrangement of her hair, she was almost sure of being told, that upon "her word she looked vastly smart, and she dared to say, would make a great many conquests."*

— Sense and Sensibility

**dovecote** A type of birdhouse with compartments for raising domesticated pigeons or doves.

Some dovecotes were large birdhouses raised on a pole, but in larger estates they were buildings constructed to accommodate hundreds of birds. The birds would leave the dovecote during the day to feed on growing crops, and then return at night, entering through a small opening in the roof. In the winter, the ground floor was covered with grain, such as corn.

Pigeons were a popular food, and were often braised, fricasseed or boiled with bacon. Both pigeons and sparrows were rolled in a flour paste and boiled as dumplings, or baked in pies.

The dovecote assured a steady food supply, especially during the winter months.

**downs**  Referring to hills. From the Celtic word, dun, meaning hill.

> The whole country about them abounded in beautiful walks. The high downs, which invited them from almost every window of the cottage to seek the exquisite enjoyment of air on their summits, were a happy alternative when the dirt of the valleys beneath shut up their superior beauties.
>
> — Sense and Sensibility

**drawing room**  The room for gathering after dinner, for music or informal dancing.

**drays**  Low, heavy carts without sides, used for hauling.

dray

## *D*

**dressed or undressed**  Formal or informal.

**duodecimo**  The size of a book, approximately 5 x 7½ inches. The term is derived from the number of leaves (a leaf is a complete page, both left and right as the book lies open) created from a standard size sheet of paper (12" x 25"). The sheet is folded over 12 times, so each sheet consists of 24 leaves or 48 pages. Most novels during Jane Austen's time were this size.

**dust**  A fuss.

*And what a dust you would have made, if I had not come!*
— Northanger Abbey

**engaged** Promised. Someone who is engaged has promised a walk or a dance.

**entail** Restrictions placed on the inheritance of land to ensure that the estate remained intact, without being sold off or split up, in order to guarantee the wealth and influence of landed families remain undiluted through generations.

> The way entail worked was that the eldest son inherited the land with the proviso that it must be handed down to his eldest son in its entirety and without mortgages. In effect, the immediate heir inherited only the income from the land, since he could not sell or divide it. However, the law only allowed the restrictions of entail

in effect until his son (the grandson of the man passing the estate) turned twenty-one. At that time, the restrictions on the land were lifted, and the inheriting grandson was free to sell it. The father could, however, sign a new deed of settlement, restricting the use of land until his grandson inherited it at age twenty-one, and so the restriction upon the land could continue in perpetuity.

If the only heirs were female, the estate could then pass laterally to a branch of the family who did have a male – the "heir apparent," as females were restricted from inheriting land. This is what happens in *Pride and Prejudice*, when Mr. Bennet's estate is inherited by Mr. Collins because "Mr. Bennet's property consisted almost entirely of an estate of two thousand a year, which, unfortunately for his daughters, was entailed in default of heirs male, on a distant relation." Similarly, a cousin of Sir Walter Elliot inherits his estate in *Persuasion*, as Sir Walter Elliot had no sons, and William Elliot is the "heir presumptive." This arrangement for passing on the family inheritance naturally made the eldest son the most desirable when it came to marriage, as younger sons would inherit nothing.

**expedition**  Speed.

*She considered it as an act of indispensable duty, to clear away the claims of creditors, with all the expedition which the most comprehensive retrenchments could secure, and saw no dignity in any thing short of it.*

—Persuasion

**extracts**  Passages copied from books.

*What say you, Mary? For you are a young lady of deep reflection, I know and read great books, and make extracts.*

—Pride and Prejudice

**fag** Tedious work, drudgery; to exhaust.

The word fag was the name given to a student at a British public school who was required to perform menial tasks for a student in a higher class. It came to mean fatiguing or tedious work.

**faggot** A bundle of twigs, sticks, or branches bound together. From the Latin *facus*, bundle. They were used as a type of match. Seven or eight sticks were used at one time, and after lighting them in the fire, they were used to light lamps and candles.

*...how much better to find a fire ready lit, than to have to wait shivering in the cold till all the*

## F

*family are in bed, as so many poor girls have been obliged to do, and then to have a faithful old servant frightening one by coming in with a faggot!*
— Northanger Abbey

**false-hangings** Tapestries concealing secret passages.

**famous** First-rate.

*...a famous ball last night, was it not?*
— Northanger Abbey

**farrier** A blacksmith, or person who shoes horses. From the Latin *ferrum*, iron.

**fender** Protective metal frame in front of a fireplace to keep hot coals and debris from falling out.

*After sitting long enough to admire every article of furniture in the room, from the sideboard to the fender, to give an account of their journey, and of all that had happened in London, Mr. Collins invited them to take a*

> *stroll in the garden, which was large and well laid out, and to the cultivation of which he attended himself.*
>
> — Pride and Prejudice

**filigree**  Delicate and intricate ornamental work made from gold, silver, or other fine, twisted wire. Also a method of cutting and rolling slim strips of paper to imitate the delicate metal-work.

**fine**  Well-dressed.

> *Dress was her passion. She had a most harmless delight in being fine; and our heroine's entrée into life could not take place till after three or four days had been spent in learning what was mostly worn, and her chaperon was provided with a dress of the newest fashion.*
>
> — Northanger Abbey

**fish** (referring to card games) Counters, similar to today's poker chips, made of ivory or bone, sometimes formed in the shape of a fish.

> Lydia talked incessantly of lottery tickets, of the fish she had lost and the fish she had won; and Mr. Collins, in describing the civility of Mr. and Mrs. Philips, protesting that he did not in the least regard his losses at whist, enumerating all the dishes at supper, and repeatedly fearing that he crowded his cousins, had more to say than he could well manage before the carriage stopped at Longbourn House.
> —Pride and Prejudice

**footman** A house servant who did chores and errands, including waiting at tables at dinner parties.

Among the responsibilities of a footman was to accompany ladies of the house when they paid calls, and he would present her calling card to the butler. His livery, or uniform, consisted of knee breeches and silk stockings. If you had two footmen, it was desirable to have them match as much as possible in height and physical characteristics.

**fortnight** Two weeks. (An alternation of 14 nights.)

**frank** (referring to posting a letter) To post a letter for free.

> Sending mail was expensive, and the cost was determined by the number of miles the letter traveled. An additional page doubled the cost. The expense was paid by the recipient of the letter, and not by the sender. Members of Parliament (M.P.s), however, could "frank" mail for free. In Mansfield Park, Edmund Bertram, aware of Fanny Price's poverty, attempts to assist her in sending a letter to her brother by suggesting her uncle, who is an M.P., send it for her.

> *...as your uncle will frank it, it will cost William nothing.*
> —Mansfield Park

**freehold property** Property owned as opposed to leased.

𝓕

**frigate**  A warship, used primarily for escort duty.

**Fullerton**  A common hired carriage.

**gapes** Fits of yawning.

> The others returned, the room filled again, benches were reclaimed and re-possessed, and another hour of pleasure or of penance as to be set out, another hour of music was to give delight or the gapes, as real or affected taste for it prevailed.
>
> —Persuasion

# G

**gig**  A lightly framed two-wheeled carriage, drawn by one horse; it was considered a fashionable carriage.

gig

**gold mohrs**  Gold coins used in British India.

**gout**  Arthritis, or swelling of the joints, thought to be caused by the consumption of too much protein. It was considered an affliction of the well to do, as the poor could not afford meat.

**Gowland**  A popular skin lotion.

**grappler**  A ship's captain.

**grazier**  One who rears and grazes cattle for market.

**great coat** A man's heavy overcoat made of wool, often with a short, layered cape or scarves attached.

**Great Nation** France.

**Gretna Green** A village in Scotland, just over the English border.

The rules regarding marriage were far more relaxed in the Scottish Presbyterian Church than the Church of England, and so when a couple wanted to elope, they went to Gretna Green, where they could marry simply by declaring their desire to marry before any witness, without the sanction of the church, or the approval of their parents. But such an undertaking was not without penalties, as the couple would be left without dowries or marriage settlements, and an elopement was considered very antisocial in a world that valued social mores.

# H

**ha-ha**  A sunken fence or wall below ground level.

What is a ha-ha wall, and why is it so funny? A ha-ha wall is a retaining wall built into a ditch, consisting of a sunken stone wall, its top level or slightly lower than the grass, and a deep, pitched ditch on the far side. It acts as an effective barrier for keeping livestock and people off property. It physically separates a lawn or garden area from neighboring property, but is designed to be invisible when viewed from the house, not only to create an uninterrupted vista, but also to trick the eye into thinking the property goes on forever. Animals on the other side of the ha-ha also appear to belong to the estate, and so visitors

*H*

gazing out over the manicured lawn would think the property extended as far as the eye could see. They were generally built in the 17th and 18th centuries on country estates of the landed gentry.

*A few steps farther brought them out at the bottom of the very walk they had been talking of; and standing back, well shaded and sheltered, and looking over a ha-ha into the park, was a comfortable-sized bench, on which they all sat down.*

—Mansfield Park

**habit** Traveling or riding clothes.

**hack chaise** A rented carriage.

**hammer** An auction, so named for the gavel being thumped when an item was sold.

**hands across** One of the movements in country-style or contra dancing.

**hanger** A wood on the side of a steep hill or bank.

> *And his woods, — I have not seen such timber any where in Dorsetshire as there is now standing in Delaford Hanger!*
> —Sense and Sensibility

**hanging wood** Forests on a hillside or slope.

> *On one side you look across the bowling-green, behind the house, to a beautiful hanging wood, and on the other you have a view of the church and village, and, beyond them, of those fine bold hills that we have so often admired.*
> —Sense and Sensibility

**hard-by** Nearby.

**hartshorn** Smelling salts made by grinding the antlers of a hart (a male deer over five years old) into powder.

*H*

> Deer antlers contain ammonia, which is the main ingredient of smelling salts.

**high** Arrogant.

> *She had long suspected the family to be very high, and this made it certain.*
>
> — Northanger Abbey

**high feathers** Plumes on hats.

> Feathers were a fashion accessory, and the larger the feather, the more expensive. Long feathers on a hat were a sign of wealth, and they were positioned upright, in order to be noticed.

> *...they saw nothing of the dancers but the high feathers of some of the ladies.*
>
> — Northanger Abbey

**hobby-horse** An obsession; a fixation. In modern days it has been shortened to hobby.

> *If he had a hobby-horse, it was that. He loved a garden.*
>
> — Northanger Abbey

**honored**  To grace with your presence.

*Have you yet honoured the Upper Rooms?*

— Northanger Abbey

**hot closets**  Drawers near the stove and chimney for keeping food warm.

*...they proceeded by quick communication to the kitchen — the ancient kitchen of the convent, rich in the massy walls and smoke of former days, and in the stoves and hot closets of the present.*

— Northanger Abbey

**hot-pressed paper**  Costly, smooth writing paper.

*Soon after their return, a letter was delivered to Miss Bennet: it came from Netherfield, and was opened immediately. The envelope contained a sheet of elegant, little, hot-pressed paper, well covered with a lady's fair, flowing hand, and Elizabeth saw her sister's countenance change as*

## H

*she read it, and saw her dwelling intently on some particular passages.*

—Pride and Prejudice

**hunters** Spirited horses trained for speed, endurance, and jumping. They were used especially for fox hunting, and were expensive to keep.

**huswife** (pronounced "huzzif") A small carrying case for needlework tools.

**innoxious**  Innocuous; not noxious or hurtful; innocent; blameless.

> Lady Dalrymple and Miss Carteret; they would soon be innoxious cousins to her.
>
> —Persuasion

**jackonet** Thin, soft muslin; a lightweight cotton cloth used for clothing and bandages.

*It would be mortifying to the feelings of many ladies, could they be made to understand how little the heart of man is affected by what is costly or new in their attire; how little it is biassed by the texture of their muslin, and how unsusceptible of peculiar tenderness towards the spotted, the sprigged, the mull or the jackonet.*

— Northanger Abbey

# J

**jade**  A broken-down horse; a nag; worn out, wearied, spiritless.

> The origin of this word is uncertain, however, it was first used in Middle English to mean "a broken-down horse." In Chaucer's *Canterbury Tales*, the host encourages the nun's priest: "Be blithe, though thou ryde upon a jade."
>
> In the early Modern English period the word for a worthless horse was often applied derogatorily to a woman considered worthless. Jaded, meaning "worn out" or "dulled by excess" is also derived from the equine jade. Originally, to jade a horse was to wear it out or break it down by overwork or abuse. It was not long before people became jaded as well. In today's modern English, it means world-weary.

**Japan** (referring to wood)  Heavy black wood, ebony.

*She took her candle and looked closely at the cabinet. It was not absolutely ebony and gold; but it was Japan, black and yellow Japan of the handsomest kind; and as she held her candle, the yellow had very much the effect of gold.*

— Northanger Abbey

**jointure** An agreement made prior to marriage, stipulating the amount a wife would receive on the death of her husband. Traditionally, it was one-third of the estate. Widows with a substantial jointure generally did not remarry, as their property would then revert to the new husband.

> *Mrs. Jennings was a widow with an ample jointure.*
> —Sense and Sensibility

**Landau**  (See barouche-landau.)

**letters of ceremony**  Formal letters informing of births, marriages, or deaths.

**liberty of the manor**  The right to hunt game on an estate.

*...but, as he was now provided with a good house and the liberty of a manor, it was doubtful*

*L*

> *to many of those who best knew the easiness of his temper, whether he might not spend the remainder of his days at Netherfield, and leave the next generation to purchase.*
>
> —Pride and Prejudice

**lieve**  Be glad to; be willing to.

> *I assure you — but my sister makes nothing of it — she was as lieve be tossed out as not.*
>
> —Persuasion

**linen-draper**  One who sells cloth.

**liveried**  Uniformed; a distinctive uniform worn by the male servants of a household.

**lodge**  A house on the grounds of a mansion, usually used for hunting or shooting parties on the estate. Some owners rented their lodges to tenants, such as Lady Russell, who lives at Kellynch Lodge on the estate of Kellynch Hall in *Persuasion*.

**loo** A card game whose object was to win the best hand out of three cards that were dealt. The losing players were required to contribute to the next pool.

**lottery tickets** A card game in which players bet that the card of one player will match that of another.

**lowness** Low spirits.

**lying-in** Giving birth and recovering.

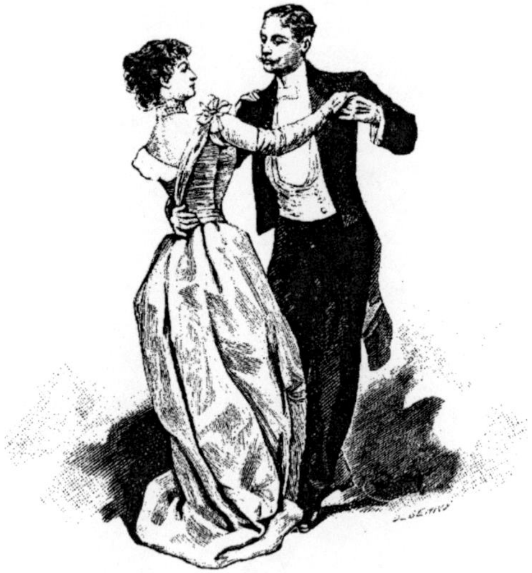

**massy** Massive.

> ...which door being only secured by massey bars and a padlock, you will, after a few efforts, succeed in opening....
> — Northanger Abbey

**Mechlin** Delicate lace made in Belgium in which the pattern details are defined by a flat thread. Mechlin is a city of north-central Belgium, north-northeast of Brussels founded in the early Middle ages, and later famous for its lace.

**meetly** Properly; fittingly.

## M

**Michaelmas** Feast of St. Michael, the Archangel, celebrated on September 29. Because it falls near the equinox, it is associated with autumn and the harvest.

**millinery** Hats.

**Molland's** A fashionable confectioner's shop in Bath.

**moonlight** The time of the month when the moon was full.

> Without electricity, traveling was difficult at night, as lanterns offered only limited illumination. Therefore, people would schedule travel and social events on nights when the moon was full.

*He hoped they would all excuse the smallness of the party, and could assure them it should never happen so again. He had been to several families that morning in hopes of procuring some addition to their number, but it was moonlight and every body was full of engagements.*

—Sense and Sensibility

**mother-in-law** Stepmother.

**muff** A cylinder-shaped cloth cover made of fur or cloth open at both ends into which the hands were placed for warmth.

> *I can hardly keep my hands warm even in my muff.*
> —Sense and Sensibility

**mull** Sheer cotton; a soft, thin muslin used in dresses and for trimmings.

**muslin** Cotton; any of various sturdy cotton fabrics of plain weave, used especially for sheets. Muslin is one of the finest kinds of cotton, very thin, and popular for dress material in Jane Austen's time.

> *Mrs. Allen congratulated herself, as soon as they were seated, on having preserved her gown from injury. "It would have been very shocking to have it torn," said she, "would not it?—It is such a delicate muslin. —For my part, I have not seen any thing I like so well in the whole room, I assure you."*
> —Northanger Abbey

## M

**mutton** Meat of an older sheep. It was also used as a synonym for dinner.

> And it all ended, at last, in his telling Henry, one morning, that when he next went to Woodston, they would take him by surprise there some day or other, and eat their mutton with him.
>
> — Northanger Abbey

**nabobs** Indian government officials with large sums of money. A person of wealth and prominence.

**needle book** A case for sewing needles, constructed to resemble a booklet.

**negus** Wine, such as sherry or port, mixed with sugar, water, lemon juice, and nutmeg. Named for its inventor, Colonel Francis Negus.

**netting** Open-mesh weaving.

**netting-box** Container for netting materials.

## N

**nunchion** (or nuncheon)  A small meal, or a snack between meals.

> Yes — I left London this morning at eight o'clock, and the only ten minutes I have spent out of my chaise since that time procured me a nunchion at Marlborough.
>
> —Sense and Sensibility

**offices** Parts of the home used for work or service, such as the kitchen, pantry, scullery, etc.

> *On each side of the entrance was a sitting room, about sixteen feet square; and beyond them were the offices and stairs.*
> 
> —Sense and Sensibility

**oiled butter** Butter that has become separated, with a thin layer of oil on top and viscous sediment at the bottom.

## O

**outrée** Extravagant.

*I never saw any thing so outrée! Those curls!*

—Emma

**outriders** Attendants riding horses alongside the chaise.

**palanquins** (pronounced "pal-en-keens") Lavishly decorated covered carriages in the East Indies, carried on poles on the shoulders of four or more bearers.

**pales** Enclosed areas.

> She supposed, if he meant any thing, he must mean an allusion to what might arise in that quarter. It distressed her a little, and she was quite glad to find herself at the gate in the pales opposite the Parsonage.
> —Pride and Prejudice

## P

**paling** A fence.

> ...but Augusta, I believe, with her own good will, would never stir beyond the park paling.
> —Emma

**Pall Mall** A fashionable street in the West End of London.

**panegyric** Elaborate public praise. From the Greek *panegurikos*, public speech.

> Catherine assented—and a very warm panegyric from her on that lady's merits, closed the subject.
> —Northanger Abbey

**panel** A piece of cloth placed under the horse's saddle that displayed the family's cote of arms.

**park** A large, enclosed landscaped area around a country estate, sometimes with grazing animals such as sheep and deer. It was constructed to provide a pleasing view from the house rather than for farming.

> Cleveland was a spacious, modern-built house, situated on a sloping lawn. It had no park, but the pleasure-grounds were

*P*

*tolerably extensive; and like every other place of the same degree of importance, it had its open shrubbery, and closer wood walk, a road of smooth gravel winding round a plantation, led to the front, the lawn was dotted over with timber, the house itself was under the guardianship of the fir, the mountain-ash, and the acacia, and a thick screen of them altogether, interspersed with tall Lombardy poplars, shut out the offices.*

—Sense and Sensibility

**patents** An open letter or document, usually from a sovereign, conferring some privilege or right. Noble titles.

**pattens** Overshoes with a high wooden sole with an iron ring on the bottom that raised the feet several inches above wet or muddy grounds. The iron ring made a clinking sound on any hard surface, especially the cobblestone streets, and were a familiar noise in the city.

> *The number of servants continually appearing, did not strike her less than the number of their offices. Wherever they went, some pattened girl stopped to curtsey, or some footman in dishabille sneaked off.*
> — Northanger Abbey

**peerage** Membership in one of the five ranks of English aristocracy: duke, marquis, earl, viscount, and baron.

**pelisse** (pronounced "pel-us") A woman's long, loose, lightweight outer cloak, often with openings for the arms. Often made of fur or with a fur lining. From the Latin *pellicius*, skin, a pelt.

> *Mrs. Allen...was forced to sit and appear to listen to all these maternal effusions, consoling herself, however, with the discovery, which her keen eyes soon made, that the lace on Mrs.*

*Thorpe's pelisse was not half so handsome as that on her own.*

— Northanger Abbey

**Pembroke** A small, four-legged table with two drop sides that could be swung up for additional space. It is believed it acquired its name when Thomas Chippendale made a table of this design for Mary Herbert, Countess of Pembroke.

**phaeton** A doorless, light, four-wheeled carriage with one or two seats, usually drawn by either one horse or a pair of horses. It was driven by the owner, with no coachman's seat.

phaeton

## P

In Greek mythology, Phaeton was the son of Helios, the god of the sun. Phaeton petitioned his father to let him drive the chariot of the sun across the sky for a single day. Bound by a promise to grant his son's one wish, Helios agreed, although not without grave concern.

His concern proved well-founded, when Phaeton, no match for the mighty horses, lost control and the fiery chariot wandered off course and flew too near the earth. It scorched the northern part of Africa, turning it to deserts and darkening the skin of the people there. Fearing that the entire earth would be burned up, Zeus was forced to destroy Phaeton with a thunderbolt.

This association of Phaeton with the speeding chariot of the sun made phaeton a good choice by coach builders as the name for a light, fast, horse-driven carriage.

**philippics** A verbal denunciation with harsh, often insulting language. Originally this term referred to the heated orations delivered by the Greek statesman Demosthenes against Phillip of Macedon in the 4th century.

**physic** To treat with medicine.

*Do not spoil them, and do not physic them.*

—Emma

**piano** Literally meaning soft in tone; soft-speaking. Figuratively meaning mild or weak.

*Well, well, ladies are the best judges; but James Benwick is rather too piano for me, and though very likely it is all our partiality, Sophy and I cannot help thinking Frederick's manners better than his.*

—Persuasion

**piano-forte** Literally "soft-loud," because its tones can be varied in loudness, unlike those of a harpsichord, the popular keyboard instrument that the piano largely replaced during Austen's lifetime.

The precursor of the piano was the harpsichord, which creates sound by a mechanism that plucks the strings, without the possibility of controlling gradations of loudness. In order to overcome this drawback, a Florentine by the name of Bartolommeo

*P*

Cristofori invented a mechanism or "action" around the year 1709, by which the strings of the instrument are struck by felt-covered hammers. This device allowed more control over the loudness of playing. Cristofori called his new instrument a *gravicembalo col piano e forte*, that is, "a harpsichord with soft and loud."

Piano means "soft" in Italian musical terminology, and forte means, "loud." Similarly, the earliest known pieces written expressly for the new instrument were sonatas that Lodovico Giustini published in 1732 for the *cembal di piano e forte ditto volgarmente di martelletti*, "the soft and loud harpsichord commonly called the one with little hammers." The instrument came to be designated by the term "piano e forte," or by contraction pianoforte, which was subsequently shortened to piano.

Broadwood's, a London manufacturer renowned for the quality of its pianofortes, was a pioneer in the technological development of the modern instrument.

**picturesque** A view in nature that resembles or suggests a suitable scene for a painting. From the Latin *pictor*, painter. The picturesque in painting and landscape gardening was in vogue in the late 18th and early 19th centuries.

*In the present instance, she confessed and lamented her want of knowledge; declared that she would give any thing in the world to be able to draw; and a lecture on the picturesque immediately followed, in which his instructions were so clear that she soon began to see beauty in every thing admired by him, and her attention was so earnest, that he became perfectly satisfied of her having a great deal of natural taste.*

— Northanger Abbey

**pin-money** An allowance given to a woman upon marriage, and part of the settlement between families of the prospective husband and wife. Money designated for a wife's private use.

**pinery** A hothouse where pineapples were grown, or a plantation that produced pineapples.

**piquet** A two-person game played with thirty-two cards.

**plaister** An alternate spelling of plaster; a bandage.

# P

**plantation** An area where cultivated trees have been planted.

> The remainder was shut off by knolls of old trees, or luxuriant plantations, and the steep woody hills rising behind to give it shelter, were beautiful even in the leafless month of March.
> — Northanger Abbey

**pocket-book** A small notebook.

> I will read you their names directly; here they are, in my pocket-book.
> — Northanger Abbey

**porter** A dark brown beer, chiefly drunk by laborers.

> A pint of porter with my cold beef at Marlborough was enough to over-set me.
> — Sense and Sensibility

**post** Short for post-chaise.

**post-chaise** A carriage led by four or six horses; an expensive and efficient mode of transportation.

post-chaise

**post-masters** Persons in charge of a station who provided lodging and fresh horses.

**postillion** A man who rides the lead horse of a pair to better control the horses.

postillion riding on lead horse

*P*

The postillion could take the place of a coachman in the case of a post-chaise, or he could assist the coachman when leading a six horse team. Postillions were usually light in weight and small in stature, like a jockey. They had their own livery that included a short, single-color jacket, a shiny white hat, white cord breeches, top-boots, a white neckcloth, and yellow waistcoat with pearl buttons. From the Italian *postiglione*, mail.

**poultice**  A cloth treated with herbs or home mixtures applied to a wound for healing purposes; a bandage.

**powdering-gown**  Garment worn to protect clothes while the hair was being powdered.

**preferment**  A church appointment or promotion that brought social or financial advantages.

> Edward's marriage with Lucy was as firmly determined on, and the time of its taking place remained as absolutely uncertain, as she had concluded it would be; — every thing depended, exactly after her expectation, on his getting that preferment, of

*P*

*which, at present, there seemed not the smallest chance.*

—Sense and Sensibility

**privateers** Vessels owned and armed by private persons who held government commissions authorized to use arms against hostile nations. They were often used for the purpose of profiteering in seized merchandise.

*I never had two days of foul weather all the time I was at sea in her; and after taking privateers enough to be very entertaining, I had the good luck, in my passage home the next autumn, to fall in with the very French frigate I wanted.*

—Persuasion

**Pump-room**  The room for pumping and drinking medicinal water. People visiting Bath, or other spa resorts, often went there for the healing properties of the medicinal water, and it often was the location for social activity during the day.

> *Every morning now brought its regular duties; — shops were to be visited; some new part of the town to be looked at; and the Pump-room to be attended, where they paraded up and down for an hour, looking at every body and speaking to no one.*
>
> — Northanger Abbey

**quadrille** A four-person game played with forty cards.

**quarto** A book made by folding whole sheets of paper twice to produce four leaves out of each original sheet.

> It was much easier to chat than to study; much pleasanter to let her imagination range and work at Harriet's fortune, than to be labouring to enlarge her comprehension, or exercise it on sober facts; and the only literary pursuit which engaged Harriet at present, the only mental provision she was making for

# Q

> *the evening of life, was the collecting and transcribing all the riddles of every sort that she could meet with, into a thin quarto of hot-pressed paper, made up by her friend, and ornamented with ciphers and trophies.*
>
> —Emma

**Queen Mab**  The fairy queen made famous in Shakespeare's play, *Romeo and Juliet.*

Queen Mab supposedly is a tiny fairy who comes to people when they sleep, and makes them dream about what they want and cannot have. In *Romeo and Juliet,* Mercutio gives the following description of her:

> O, then, I see Queen Mab hath been with you.
> She is the fairies' midwife, and she comes
> In shape no bigger than an agate-stone
> On the fore-finger of an alderman,
> Drawn with a team of little atomies
> Over men's noses as they lie asleep;
> Her chariot is an empty hazel-nut
> Made by the joiner squirrel or old grub,
> Time out o' mind the fairies' coachmakers.
> Her wagon-spokes made of long spinners' legs,
> The cover of the wings of grasshoppers,
> The traces of the smallest spider's web,
> The collars of the moonshine's watery beams,
> Her whip of cricket's bone, the lash of film,

Her wagoner a small grey-coated gnat,
Not so big as a round little worm
Prick'd from the lazy finger of a maid;
And in this state she gallops night by night
Through lovers' brains, and then they dream of love;
O'er courtiers' knees, that dream on court'sies straight,
O'er lawyers' fingers, who straight dream on fees,
O'er ladies ' lips, who straight on kisses dream,
Which oft the angry Mab with blisters plagues,
Because their breaths with sweetmeats tainted are:
Sometime she gallops o'er a courtier's nose,
And then dreams he of smelling out a suit;
And sometime comes she with a tithe-pig's tail
Tickling a parson's nose as a' lies asleep,
Then dreams, he of another benefice:
Sometime she driveth o'er a soldier's neck,
And then dreams he of cutting foreign throats,
Of breaches, ambuscadoes, Spanish blades,
Of healths five-fathom deep; and then anon
Drums in his ear, at which he starts and wakes,
And being thus frighted swears a prayer or two
And sleeps again. This is that very Mab
That plaits the manes of horses in the night,
And bakes the elflocks in foul sluttish hairs,
Which once untangled, much misfortune bodes:
This is the hag, when maids lie on their backs,
That presses them and learns them first to bear,
Making them women of good carriage:
This is she—

# Q

*When you leave Barton to form your own establishment in a more last home, Queen Mab shall receive you.*

— Sense and Sensibility

**quiz** A bizarre or unusual object.

*"Ah, mother! How do you do?" said he, giving her a hearty shake of the hand: "where did you get that quiz of a hat, it makes you look like an old witch?"*

— Northanger Abbey

**quizzes** Eccentric or teasing people.

The origin of the word quiz is unknown, however, the first recorded use of the word was associated with people, and not tests. In 1782, quiz meant "an odd or eccentric person." From the noun came a verb meaning "to make sport or fun of" and "to regard mockingly." In English dialects and in American English the verb quiz began to acquire meanings relating to

*Q*

interrogation and questioning. This presumably occurred because quiz was associated with question, inquisitive, inquisition, or perhaps the English dialect verb quiset, "to question," probably itself short for obsolete inquisite, "to investigate." From this new meaning came the noun and verb, whose meaning is all too familiar to students.

> ...then let us walk about and quiz people. Come along with me, and I will shew you the four greatest quizzers in the room; my two younger sisters and their partners. I have been laughing at them this half hour.
> — Northanger Abbey

**raillery** Mild or good-natured teasing or ridicule.

*...but she was not experienced enough in the finesse of love, or the duties of friendship, to know when delicate raillery was properly called for; or when a confidence should be forced.*
— Northanger Abbey

**(the) Rambler** A periodical published by Samuel Johnson between 1750 and 1752. Its topics dealt with miscellaneous subjects, ranging from literary criticism to character study.

## R

**Ramsgate**  Seaside resort on the English Channel.

**rattle**  To talk rapidly in a thoughtless or noisy manner. To chatter tediously. A chatterbox.

> *He is as good-natured a fellow as ever lived; a little of a rattle; but that will recommend him to your sex I believe....?*
>
> —Northanger Abbey

**recreating** (oneself)  Restoring or recovering from work or exhaustion.

> *Mrs. Jennings, knowing nothing of any change in the patient, went unusually early to bed; her maid, who was one of the principal nurses, was recreating herself in the housekeeper's room, and Elinor remained alone with Marianne.*
>
> —Sense and Sensibility

**red gum**  An inflammation of the gums from teething.

**Regulars**  Soldiers in the regular army, as opposed to the militia which were volunteer soldiers. The regular army was more prestigious than the militia.

**rencontre**  Encounter (French).

> The story told well: he had not thrown himself away — he had gained a woman of 10,000*l*., or thereabouts, and he had gained her with such delightful rapidity; the first hour of introduction had been so very soon followed by distinguishing notice; the history which he had to give Mrs. Cole of the rise and progress of the affair was so glorious; the steps so quick, from the accidental recontre, to the dinner at Mr. Green's, and the party at Mrs. Brown's, — smiles and blushes rising in importance, — with consciousness and agitation richly scattered; the lady had been so easily impressed, — so sweetly disposed; — had, in short, to use a most intelligible phrase, been so very ready to have him, that vanity and prudence were equally contented.
>
> —*Emma*

## R

**reticule** A woman's drawstring bag for personal items. The close-fitting dresses that were the fashion of the day were made without pockets, necessitating small purses to carry personal items.

**retrench** To cut down or reduce; to remove, delete, or omit; to curtail expenses, economize. From the French *retrenchier*, to cut.

**romancers** Fiction writers.

> ...it is not a trifle that will support a family now-a-days; and after all that romancers may say, there is no doing without money.
>
> — Northanger Abbey

**rout-cakes** Sweet cakes made specifically for parties.

> She was a little shocked at the want of two drawing-rooms, at the poor attempt at rout-cakes, and there being no ice in the Highbury card parties.
>
> — Emma

**saloon** Elegant living room.

> On reaching the house, they were shown through the hall into the saloon, whose northern aspect rendered it delightful for summer.
>
> —Pride and Prejudice

**sampler** A decorative piece of needlework with letters or verses embroidered in various types of stitches to show skill.

**sarsenet or sarcenet**  A fine, soft, thin silk, often used in linings. From the Latin *saracenus*, flesh.

> *I remember too, Miss Andrews drank tea with us that evening, and wore her puce-coloured sarsenet; and she looked so heavenly, that I thought your brother must certainly fall in love with her; I could not sleep a wink all night for thinking of it.—*
>
> —Northanger Abbey

**Scarborough**  A fashionable coastal resort town in northern England.

**scrape**  A bow while drawing back one foot along the ground.

> *John Thorpe, who in the mean time, had been giving orders about the horses, soon joined them, and from him she directly received the amends which were her due; for while he slightly and carelessly touched the hand of Isabella, on her he bestowed a*

*whole scrape and half a short bow.*

— Northanger Abbey

**screen (or fire screen)** A screen placed in front of the fireplace to protect the floor from sparks and flying embers. It was also used to shield guests sitting near the fire from excessive heat. It was a pastime in Jane Austen's time for ladies to create decorative paintings on them. In *Sense and Sensibility*, Elinor Dashwood

*...painted a very pretty pair of screens for her sister-in-law, which being now just mounted and brought home, ornamented her present drawing-room.*

— Sense and Sensibility

**(the) season** The London social season of balls, parties, and sporting events that extended from May through July. During this time, the city was bustling with nobility and the upper classes.

*Mrs. Allen was so long in dressing, that they did not enter*

*S*

> *the ball-room till late. The season was full, the room crowded, and the two ladies squeezed in as well as they could.*
>
> —Northanger Abbey

**se'night** (also se'nnight) A week (a contraction of seven nights).

**sessions** Period in which a court was in operation.

**set** The basic formation in the dance.

**setting your cap** Determining to gain the attention or affection of a man.

> *You will be setting your cap at him now, and never think of poor Brandon.*
>
> —Sense and Sensibility

**shoe-roses** Ornamental ribbons worn on shoes.

**sink** To faint.

> *Mrs. Taylor told me of it half an hour ago, and she was told it by a particular friend of Miss Grey herself, else I am sure I should not have believed it; and I was almost ready to sink as it was.*
>
> —Sense and Sensibility

**sitting room** Room used for morning activities, such as letter writing, reading, or sewing. Often a husband would work in the study, while his wife used the sitting room.

**sloop** A single-masted sailing boat.

**spars** Souvenirs; ornaments made from crystalline minerals.

**(the) Spectator** A daily paper supposedly written by Mr. Spectator, a fictitious Londoner, who wrote about popular literature, society, and morals. It was in fact written by Joseph Addison and Richard Steele, and was only in existence from March 1711 until December 1712.

**speculation** (card game) A round game in which players ante up, draw cards, and then buy and sell them to try to make the highest trump.

> *What shall I do, Sir Thomas? Whist and speculation; which will amuse me most?*
>
> —Mansfield Park

**spencer** A short jacket; a close-fitting waist-length jacket. Named after George John Spencer, Second Earl of Spencer 1758-1834.

**spinet** One of the smaller keyboard instruments that were manufactured in the course of the development of the modern piano; today the term refers specifically to a small and compact upright piano.

> *...and there is poor Jane Fairfax, who is mistress of music, has not any thing of the nature of an*

> *instrument, not even the pitifulest old spinet in the world, to amuse herself with.*
> — Emma

**splash-board**  A panel on carriages to protect against splashes.

**sprigged muslin**  Cotton fabric with a leaf or small flower design.

**spunging-house**  Place where debtors were sent in an attempt to collect payments for their debts before they were locked up in debtor's prison. A place of preliminary confinement for debtors.

> *Regard for a former servant of my own, who had since fallen into misfortune, carried me to visit him in a spunging-house, where he was confined for debt; and there, in the same house, under a similar confinement, was my unfortunate sister.*
> — Sense and Sensibility

**squire**  Member of the gentry below a knight and above a gentleman; the principal landowner in a district.

**steward** The manager of an estate.

**stewponds** Fish ponds kept by manor houses to ensure a supply of fresh fish.

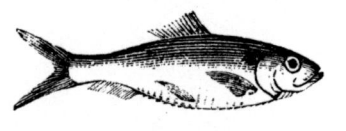

**stops** Periods in a sentence.

*As far as I have had opportunity of judging, it appears to me that the usual style of letter-writing among women is faultless, except in three particulars.... A general deficiency of subject, a total inattention to stops, and a very frequent ignorance of grammar."*
— Northanger Abbey

**succession-houses** Hothouses.

**sweep** A winding drive.

**sweep-gate** The main entry gate to the house, attached to the wall around the property.

**tambour** A small wooden embroidery frame consisting of two concentric hoops between which fabric is stretched.

**Tattersals's** A well-known resort for betting and auctioning horses.

**Temple** An area of London.
> Two Inns of the Court were located in this district of London, and lawyers and students often leased rooms in this part of town. The site of the property was once the seat of the Knights Templar.

## T

> *He was then the inferior in circumstances, he was then the poor one; he had chambers in the Temple, and it was as much as he could do to support the appearance of a gentleman.*
>
> — Persuasion

**tenements** Rented dwellings.

**tickets** Calling cards.

> Among the complex rules of social etiquette in Jane Austen's time was the presentation of calling cards. Women would drive around to the homes of individuals they would like to visit, or with whom they would like to develop a social relationship, and their footman would leave their card with the butler, who would then place their card on a table in the front hall or on the mantelpiece, visible to visitors who could then be impressed by their acquaintances. Having received a calling card, it was then incumbent upon the recipient to return a calling card, or better, pay an actual visit.
>
> Instead of merely leaving your calling card, you could, of course, inquire as to whether the lady of the house was at home. The butler would then present your card to his mistress,

and await her reply as to whether she was at home or not. It was understood that the lady of the house could be physically at home, but not "socially" at home, and was therefore not obliged to entertain her visitor. However, to be so rejected could be mortifying, and by simply leaving your card you did not risk such a rebuff.

In *Northanger Abbey*, Catherine Morland calls upon Miss Tilney, inquiring if Miss Tilney is at home. She is told by the man who answers the door that he thinks she is at home, but is not certain, and asks her if she would like to present her card. He returns a few minutes later to inform her that he had been mistaken, and Miss Tilney is not at home.

*Catherine, with a blush of mortification, left the house. She left almost persuaded that Miss Tilney was at home, and too much offended to admit her; and as she retired down the street could not withhold one glance at the drawing-room windows, in expectation of seeing her there, but no one appeared at them. At the bottom of the street, however, she looked back again, and then, not at a window, but issuing from the door, she saw Miss Tilney herself.*

— Northanger Abbey

**tippet**  A shoulder cape, often of fur or cloth, with long ends that hung in front. They were often made of minks or foxes, and the tail and paws would hang down over the shoulders.

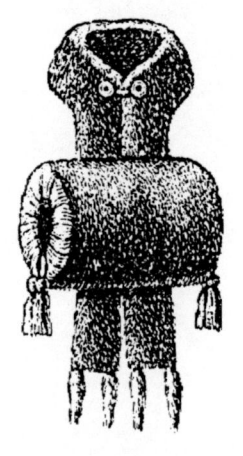

muff and tippet

**tittle-tattle**  Gossip.

*The attentions of a certain person can hardly be among the tittle-tattle of Highbury yet.*

— Emma

**tittuppy** Rickety; also, to move in a lively, prancing manner. (Perhaps imitative of the sound of a horse's hooves.)

> Oh, lord! Did you ever see such a tittuppy thing in your life? There is not a sound piece of iron about it. The wheels have been fairly worn out these ten years at least—and as for the body! Upon my soul, you might shake it to pieces yourself with a touch!
> —Northanger Abbey

**top of the room** The far end, where tiers of benches overlooked the dance floor.

**town-built** Made in London.

**trophies** An ornamental or symbolic grouping of objects. Inscriptions.

**tunbridge-ware box** Decorative boxes inlaid with wood mosaics, made by artisans in Tunbridge Wells, Kent, England.

> Tunbridge Ware is a type of decorative, inlaid mosaic woodwork, produced by local artisans from the area of Tunbridge Wells in Kent beginning in the 18th century. The wooden mosaic was created using many very small

pieces of different types and colors of wood. Shaped rods and slivers of wood were carefully glued together, and then cut into many thin slices with a fine saw. The skill was in knowing how to stack the wood layers to create a pictorial vignette. The most creative Tunbridge Ware makers used as many as 160 different woods, most of them rare or exotic, to achieve the different colors that are seen in their mosaics. All the colors are natural, with no dyes used.

Tunbridge Ware was utilitarian as well as decorative, and a far from exhaustive list includes boxes of many sizes and purposes, as well as small tables, writing desks, music stands, cribbage, chess, and backgammon boards, sewing thimbles, needle cases, book ends, and earrings. It reached the peak of its popularity during the 19th century, and the young Princess Victoria reputedly bought many pieces as gifts. In 1826, the town of Tunbridge Wells gave Victoria a work table, veneered with woods from every part of the globe.

In 1939, Tunbridge Ware was last manufactured commercially, although there are still a few skilled craftsmen who keep the technique alive. The town of Tunbridge Wells has an extensive and impressive collection of Tunbridge Ware on display at the Tunbridge

Wells Museum and Art Gallery in the center of town.

*Within abundance of silver paper was a pretty little tunbridge-ware box, which Harriet opened: it was well lined with the softest cotton; but, excepting the cotton, Emma saw only a small piece of court-plaister.*

— Emma

**tumble** Rumple.

*My dear, you tumble my gown.*
— Northanger Abbey

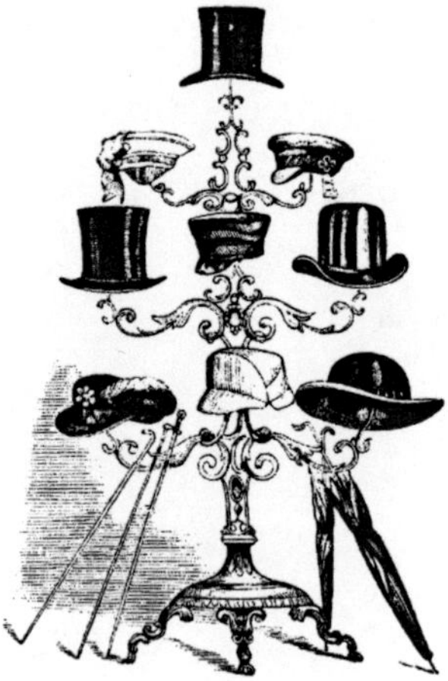

**uncensured**  Free of criticism.

**unexceptionable**  Adequate, satisfactory.

**upper assembly rooms**  Place where visitors to Bath would gather to socialize.

**vingt-un (or ving-et-un)**  Card game twenty-one, or blackjack, where the players attempt to get as close to twenty-one without exceeding that number.

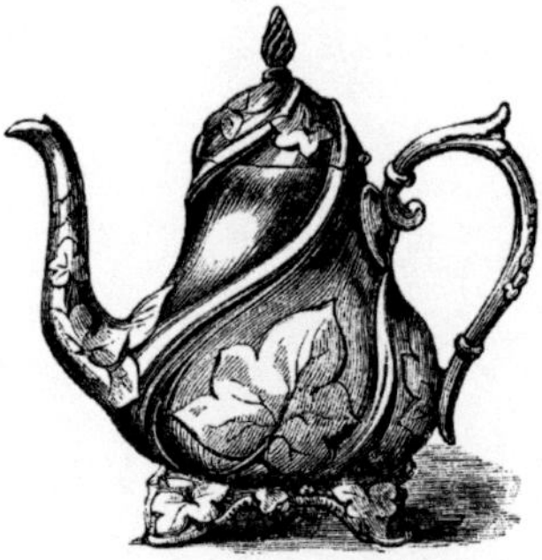

**waistcoats** Sleeveless garments for gentlemen worn under a suit coat. They were generally made of fine cotton, wool, or silk. A flannel waistcost, such as Colonel Brandon wears in *Sense and Sensibility*, gives the impression of being common and unfashionable.

**waited on** Made a formal call on.

**ward** A child under protection or custody.

> In modern times, we think of a ward as an unfortunate child, who, through misfortune, ends up in the care of the state or an institution. However, in Jane Austen's time, it was not unusual for children to be sent to live with relatives or friends. Jane's own brother, Edward,

# W

was adopted by distant cousins, Thomas Knight and his new bride. They became very fond of Edward when they visited the Austen parsonage shortly after their marriage in 1779. When they were ready to continue on their honeymoon travels, they asked permission to take Edward with them. They were childless, and so great was their affection for Edward, that they ultimately adopted him, and as they were quite wealthy, he inherited their fortune. He did, however, continue to remain close to the Austen family throughout his life. Jane was very fond of Mrs. Knight, as well. Mrs. Knight became Jane's patron, giving her an annual allowance, and it was ultimately Edward's inheritance that allowed Jane to live at the house in Chawton where she did most of her writing.

**warehouse** A dignified term for a shop.

*She could soon tell at what coach-maker's the new carriage was building, by what painter Mr. Willoughby's portrait was drawn, and at what warehouse Miss Grey's clothes might be seen.*

— Sense and Sensibility

**whip hand**  The hand that holds the whip while driving or riding. Figuratively, it means to have control, or to have the upper hand.

> "Aye, you may abuse me as you please," said the good-natured old lady, "you have taken Charlotte off my hands, and cannot give her back again. So there I have the whip hand of you."
> —Sense and Sensibility

**whist**  Card game resembling bridge, played by two sets of partners.

**white soup**  Gravy, egg yolks, almonds, cream, and negus (sweet and spiced wine with water), commonly served at a ball.

**wilderness** (in reference to a garden) Part of a garden or park that had trees in it, sometimes planted to look uncultivated, and sometimes planted in a kind of maze.

> "James," said Mrs. Rushworth to her son, "I believe the wilderness will be new to all the

# W

> party. The Miss. Bertrams have never seen the wilderness yet."
>
> —Mansfield Park

**workbags** Bags for needlework.

> As soon as all had ate, and the elder ones paid, the carriage was ordered; and, after some contrivance, the whole party, with all their boxes, workbags, and parcels, and the unwelcome addition of Kitty's and Lydia's purchases, were seated in it.
>
> —Pride and Prejudice

**worsting** Getting worse.

> Anne haggard, Mary coarse, every face in the neighbourhood worsting; and the rapid increase of the crow's foot about Lady Russell's temples had long been a distress to him.
>
> —Persuasion

**younker** Youngster.

# Chronology

| | |
|---|---|
| 1775 | Jane Austen was born on December 16 in the Parsonage at Steventon, Hampshire, the seventh of eight children (two girls and six boys). She would become very close to her only sister, Cassandra, and they would live together until her death. |
| 1783 | Jane and Cassandra attended Mrs. Cawley's school in Oxford, which later moved to Southampton. |
| 1785-86 | Jane and Cassandra boarded at the Abbey School in Reading, which is believed to have been the model for Mrs. Goddard's school in *Emma*. |
| 1787 | Between the ages of 12 and 16, Jane began writing short, fictional works, which would become known as her *Juvenilia*. |
| 1792 | Cassandra became engaged to the Rev. Mr. Tom Fowle, who later died of tropical fever in the West Indies in 1797. |
| 1794-95 | Austen wrote the epistolary* version of *Elinor and Marianne*, which would later be revised as *Sense and Sensibility*. |

*novel of letters

| | |
|---|---|
| 1796 | Austen began writing *First Impressions*, also in the epistolary style. This was the first version of *Pride and Prejudice*. |
| 1797 | Austen completed *First Impressions*. Her father contacted the London publisher, Cadell and Company, but his letter was returned unopened. In November, Austen began revising *Elinor and Marianne* as *Sense and Sensibility*. |
| 1798 | Austen wrote *Susan*, the first version of *Northanger Abbey*. |
| 1801 | Jane's father retired and the family left the quiet life of Steventon, and moved to Bath, where they resided until 1806. Bath would become partial settings for both *Northanger Abbey* and *Persuasion*. |
| 1803 | Jane's novel, *Susan*, was sold to the publisher Crosby & Company in London for £10 but they never published it. |
| 1804 | Jane wrote, *The Watsons*, a novel that was never finished. |
| 1805 | Her father, the Reverend George Austen, died, and the following year she moved to Southampton with her mother and sister. |
| 1809 | After many short-term stays at various residences, the three women settled at Chawton Cottage in Hampshire, through the largess of her brother, Edward. It was here that Jane wrote and revised her most famous works. |

| | |
|---|---|
| 1811 | In March, Austen began writing *Mansfield Park*, and in November, *Sense and Sensibility* was published "By a Lady." All of her subsequent novels would be published anonymously. |
| 1812 | *First Impressions* was revised and sold to the publisher Edgerton for £110. |
| 1813 | *Pride and Prejudice* was published, and went through two editions in one year. |
| 1814 | Austen wrote *Emma*, and *Mansfield Park* was published. |
| 1815 | Austen completed *Emma*, and began writing *Persuasion*. |
| 1816 | *Emma* was published. Her brother, Henry, bought back *Susan* from the publisher for the original £10, and Austen revised it as *Northanger Abbey*. |
| 1817 | Austen began writing *Sandition*, a satirical novel about hypochondriacs and health spas, but it was not finished because of her declining health. She and Cassandra traveled to Winchester for medical care, but Jane Austen died there on July 18 at age 42 from Addison's disease (a disorder of the adrenal gland). She is buried in Winchester Cathedral.

*Northanger Abbey* and *Persuasion* were published in December through the efforts of her brother, Henry (although 1818 is printed as the year of publication). In the "Biographical Notice," Henry identified |

Jane Austen as the author of these works, as well as *Sense and Sensibility*, *Pride and Prejudice*, *Mansfield Park*, and *Emma*.

# Bibliography

Austen, Jane, *Emma*. New York, NY: Barnes & Noble Classics, 2004. (First published in 1816.)

———, *Mansfield Park*. New York, NY: Barnes & Noble Classics, 2004. (First published in three volumes in 1814.)

———, *Northanger Abbey*. New York, NY: Barnes & Noble Classics, 2005. (First published posthumously in 1818.)

———, *Persuasion*. New York, NY: Barnes & Noble Classics, 2003. (First published posthumously in 1818.)

———, *Pride and Prejudice*. New York, NY: Barnes & Noble Classics, 2003. (First published in 1813.)

———, *Sense and Sensibility*. New York, NY: Barnes & Noble Classics, 2002. (First published in 1811.)

———, *Sense and Sensibility*. New York: NY, W. W. Norton & Company, Inc., 2002.

Austen-Leigh, J.E., *A Memoir of Jane Austen*, New York, NY: Oxford University Press, 2002.

Byrde, Penelope, *Jane Austen Fashion*. Great Britain, Twickenham, Middlesex, 1999.

Hannon, Patrice, *101 Things You Didn't Know About Jane Austen*. Avon, MA: Adams Media, 2007.

Le Faye, Deirdre, *Jane Austen: The World of Her Novels*. London: Frances Lincoln Limited, 2002.

*The Merriam-Webster New Book of Word Histories*, Springfield, MA: Merriam-Webster Inc., Publishers, 1991.

*Oxford English Dictionary, 2nd Edition*, prepared by J. A. Simpson and B. S. C. Weiner. Oxford University Press, 1989.

Pool, Daniel, *What Jane Austen Ate and Charles Dickens Knew*. New York, NY: Touchstone, 1993.

Ray, Joan Klingel, Ph.D., *Jane Austen for Dummies*. Indianapolis, IN: Wiley Publishing, Inc., 2006.

Shields, Carol, *Jane Austen*. New York, NY: Penguin Group, 2001.

Tomalin, Claire, *Jane Austen: A Life*. New York, NY: Vintage Books, a division of Random House, Inc., 1999.

White, R.J., *Life in Regency England*. London: B.T. Batsford Ltd., 1963.

## Jane Austen Font

Pia Frauss is the designer of this beautiful font which is made up of characters penned by Jane Austen. Although the text is not an exact replication of her original writings, it allows us to view the quoted material in this book in a close approximation of her handwriting. It is used with permission.